Excel
Basic Skills

AF751510

Basic Reading Skills

3–4 Years

Ages 8-10

Get the Results You Want!

PASCAL PRESS

Peter Howard

Reprinted 2006, 2007, 2008, 2009, 2011, 2012, 2013, 2014, 2016, 2017, 2019, 2020, 2022, 2025

ISBN 978 1 74125 166 1

Pascal Press
PO Box 250
Glebe NSW 2037
(02) 9198 1748
www.pascalpress.com.au

Publisher: Vivienne Joannou
Edited by Christine Eslick
Illustrations by Art Explosion
Page layout and typesetting by Typecellars Pty Ltd
Cover by DiZign Pty Ltd
Printed by Vivar Printing/Green Giant Press

Contents

Introduction

In today's world, most children probably read less than their parents or grandparents did at the same age. Distractions such as television and video games take up many hours that could be spent in reading. To excel in reading requires plenty of practice.

The **Excel Basic Skills: Basic Reading Skills** series is a three-book set of workbooks for Years 1-2, 3-4 and 5-6 which aims to give primary school children this important practice in reading and understanding using a variety of accessible texts. Each varied one-page exercise should not take more than about **15 minutes**. Most pages have questions that require one-word answers. These words are found in the text or on the page. This ensures that a child must concentrate hard and read every word.

In this second book in the series, **Basic Reading Skills Years 3-4**, the activities cover a wide range of reading skills such as:

- basic comprehension of a text
- predicting words in a story
- recognising different 'voices' in a text
- finding words that are wrong
- sorting different kinds of words.

Fun activities, such as anagram puzzles and simple crosswords, are also included.

Parents and teachers are advised to remove the answers from the centre of the book. When correcting a child's work, it is important to explain any errors that have been made.

Greed causes everyone to suffer

One day a dog was out for a walk. He became tired, so when he came to a farm, he entered the barn. Then he jumped into a manger, which is a box where hay is stored for cattle or horses. This manger was full of hay and the dog wanted to rest before he continued his journey.

After a while an ox came up to the manger and wanted to eat some hay. The dog sprang up and barked furiously. The ox tried and tried again, but the dog snarled and showed its teeth.

The ox said, 'Why will you not let me eat my hay? It is of no use to you as you cannot eat hay like I do.'

'That doesn't matter,' snarled the dog. 'If I can't eat it myself, nobody else shall have it.'

Tick the box against each sentence that is true.

1 The dog wanted to sleep in the manger. ☐

2 The manger was full of corn. ☐

3 An ox came to the manger to feed. ☐

4 The dog would not let the ox eat a thing. ☐

5 The ox said that the dog could share the food with him. ☐

6 In the end the dog agreed to let the ox eat. ☐

How deep is the sea?

The sea varies in depth as much as the land varies in height. There are slopes that descend gradually from the shore. Sometimes there are plains and tablelands that run for many kilometres at the same depth.

Besides these fairly shallow areas, there are precipices with sheer descents into chasms that are up to ten thousand metres deep. The deepest part of all the oceans is just south of the Philippines.

It is interesting to remember how depths were once measured. A leaden weight on a huge reel of very fine wire was lowered into the sea. Today supersonic sound waves can be aimed from a ship down to the sea bed. A signal is reflected back to the ship giving the exact depth below.

Use a word from the story to fill each space.

1 The sea bed has ups and downs as does the ____________.

2 A steep drop in the ocean, as on land, is a ______________.

3 The deepest part of the sea is near the ________________.

4 What kind of sound waves measure water depth? ___________

5 Which word means the same as **changes**? ______________

6 Which word means the opposite of **approximate**? __________

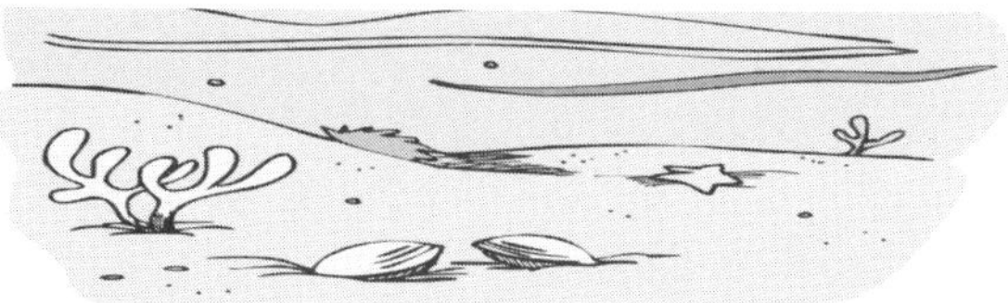

Missing words 1

One word is missing in each line where there are four dots. Write the word that you think should be there.

Ned Kelly is Australia's most w.... known	1	______________
bushranger. He and his g.... rode on	2	______________
horseback, stealing m.... and valuables.	3	______________
Finally the gang was surrounded by p...	4	______________
in 1881 at Glenrowan. There was a f....	5	______________
shootout. Ned and two of his m... wore	6	______________
armour made from old pieces of i.... . No	7	______________
bullet pierced Ned's armour, but he w....	8	______________
wounded in o.... leg and in both arms.	9	______________
Finally the police m.... in and captured	10	______________
the badly w.... bushranger. He was	11	______________
treated in h.... before his trial. The judge	12	______________
found him g.... of murder and sentenced	13	______________
him to d.... by hanging in Melbourne.	14	______________

Can bats see in the dark?

There is something about bats that we cannot understand. How do they fly in the dark without bumping into things? A scientist turned a bat loose in a pitch dark room. Obstacles were placed around, including ropes that dangled from the ceiling. The bat simply flew round and round without touching a thing, including the walls.

We now think that a cluster of nerves on a bat's nose acts like radar. These nerves send signals that bounce back from objects.

Most bats are harmless. Some eat only insects, others only fruit. The rare vampire bats are a real pest. They attack animals, especially cattle and poultry. They may attack humans. By biting a tiny hole in the flesh, these bats suck blood from the victim. They do not take enough blood to kill, but they can pass on a fatal disease called rabies.

Use a word from the story to fill each space.

1 Bats avoid objects when they fly in the ____________.

2 We think nose nerves act like ________________.

3 Most bats eat __________________ or insects.

4 Rabies is a disease passed on by ______________ bats.

5 Which word means the same as **bunch**? ________________

6 Which word means the opposite of **spit**? ________________

What happened to Pompeii?

Pompeii was a Roman city with about 20 000 people. In AD 79 – nearly two thousand years ago – a nearby volcano named Vesuvius erupted. Streams of lava, mud, stones and ashes covered the city.

When the molten debris had dried out, the city was sealed. It was as if a giant pie had been made – the city lay in the middle of a thick crust.

The city of Pompeii was buried beneath the lava and ashes for over one thousand five hundred years. Digging began some three hundred years ago, but most progress took place last century. Today a visitor can walk down streets and into houses that are nearly two thousand years old. There is a museum nearby. Many household items and bodies covered with lava have been preserved.

Use a word from the story to fill each space.

1 The name of a volcano was ____________.

2 The city that became buried was ________________.

3 Today you can see many old houses and ________________.

4 There is a ______________ which has items used by Romans.

5 Which word means the same as **huge**? ________________

6 Which word means the opposite of **solid**? ________________

Who is speaking? 1

Read each sentence. Write who is speaking in the space. Choose answers from the box.

pirate	groom	barber	magician	acrobat
police officer	keeper	usher	burglar	violinist

1 This gorilla looks friendly, but he can turn nasty. ____________

2 Now, with one tap of my wand, the egg is gone! ____________

3 Your seat is the fifth one along this row. ____________

4 Hurry, you men! Bury the treasure before sunset. ____________

5 May I see your licence, driver? ____________

6 This safe is proving difficult to crack. ____________

7 Would you like me to take more off the top? ____________

8 I was injured doing a double somersault. ____________

9 The conductor praised my solo effort. ____________

10 The mare's coat needs a good brushing. ____________

Easier said than done

Some mice lived in a house where there was a fierce cat. Even in the dark they dared not stir. They could easily be pounced upon. It was becoming harder and harder to go out to find food. One day they all met together to talk over a plan.

'I will tell you what to do,' said a young mouse. 'It is quite easy. Tie a bell around the cat's neck. When the cat walks, the bell will ring, and we will know where he is.'

The other mice squeaked with joy. Then an old mouse spoke out. 'But who is going to put the bell around the cat's neck?' he asked.

They all looked at each other. Nobody offered to do it.

Tick the box against each sentence that is true.

1 The cat only came out after dark. ☐

2 The mice were all afraid of the cat. ☐

3 At the meeting an old mouse wanted to use a bell. ☐

4 The young mouse said the cat would like a bell. ☐

5 Everyone thought the bell was a good idea. ☐

6 The problem was how to put the bell on the cat. ☐

Who studied germs?

Just over 150 years ago winemakers in France were upset. Much of their wine, which they had stored away, was going sour before it could be sold. They asked Louis Pasteur, who was a professor at a university, to solve the problem.

This clever man was interested in germs. He used a microscope and found that it was germs that spoilt the wine. He experimented and found that the germs could be killed by heating the wine for a few minutes. This cured the problem and did not harm the wine.

Pasteur spent his whole life studying germs. He found that heating milk meant it could stay fresh longer. This process is called pasteurisation today. He found that germs were the cause of many diseases.

Use a word from the story to fill each space.

1 Wine made in ____________ was turning sour.

2 Pasteur found that ________________ caused the problem.

3 This was cured by ________________ the wine.

4 What process has been named after Pasteur? ______________

5 Which word means the same as **discovered**? ______________

6 Which word means the opposite of **sweet**? ________________

Missing words 2

One word is missing in each line where there are four dots. Write the word that you think should be there.

There are about four hundred d.... 1 ____________

k.... of sharks in the world's oceans. 2 ____________

Some are as s.... as your foot and others 3 ____________

are almost the s.... of whales. 4 ____________

Sharks do not have bones as f.... do. 5 ____________

Instead, the skeleton is m.... up of cartilage 6 ____________

– rather l.... the inside of your nose. 7 ____________

The great white s.... is the largest that 8 ____________

hunts prey. Its favourite meal is a f.... seal. 9 ____________

An abalone diver has to w.... out as this 10 ____________

shark may think he is a s.... . 11 ____________

Luckily, megalodon, a shark far l.... and 12 ____________

fiercer than the great white d.... out two 13 ____________

million years ago. It was a terror of the s.... 14 ____________

Who were the Beatles?

'The Beatles' was the name of a famous group of pop stars. Four young men from Liverpool, England, formed the group in 1960. They all had the same kind of haircut. The style is still known as the 'Beatle cut'.

The four were John Lennon, Paul McCartney, George Harrison and the drummer, Ringo Starr.

The Beatles sang their own songs. They were spotted by a man who owned a record shop, and he took over the job of managing this new group. Among the first singles released were 'Love Me Do' and 'I Want to Hold Your Hand'. In America these songs topped the charts and sales around the world grew and grew. The group also appeared in films and concerts. They became very rich and decided to split up in 1970.

Use a word from the story to fill each space.

1 The Beatles were from the city of ______________.

2 The last name of the drummer was ___________________.

3 The Beatles' manager owned a ____________________ shop.

4 Which country besides England is mentioned? ______________

5 Which word means the same as **noticed**? __________________

6 Which word means the opposite of **poor**? __________________

Who is speaking? 2

Read each sentence. Write who is speaking in the space. Choose answers from the box.

minister jeweller optician smuggler builder
spy ballerina doorman matador detective

1 Check this beer glass for fingerprints. ______________

2 I must steal plans of the new fighter aircraft. ______________

3 The pearls in this necklace are real ones. ______________

4 Yes, sir, I'll call a cab for you straight away. ______________

5 I will try not to look nervous at the airport. ______________

6 These glasses suit the shape of your face. ______________

7 Watch this bull, as he looks angry to me. ______________

8 Do you want concrete or wooden steps? ______________

9 I now pronounce you husband and wife. ______________

10 My legs felt tired after so much dancing. ______________

How does a plane land?

Let us look at a small plane with a single engine. It is flying straight and the pilot sees the airport in the distance. Pretend you are the pilot. You want to land. Your first job is to lose power. To do this, you must start to close the throttle and at the same time move the control stick forward so the nose of the plane is pointing downward.

Now you are gliding, but you must still steer the plane with your feet on the rudders. Line up the nose with the runway. When you get near enough to the ground you can close the throttle further and pull the control stick back. This will slow the plane down and bring the nose up so it is no longer gliding. It is dropping or – to use the correct term – it is stalling. The plane should sink to the ground and the wheels run along the runway. You now use your brakes to come to a stop.

Use a word from the story to fill each space.

1 To lose power you must close the ________________.

2 A plane is steered by using the ________________.

3 A plane that drops with no power is ________________.

4 What stops a plane on the ground? ________________

5 Which word means the same as **one**? ________________

6 Which word means the opposite of **push**? ________________

There are all kinds of treasure

An old farmer who was about to die called his two sons and said: 'My boys, all the fortune that I have is in my farmhouse and fields. I am giving all this to you in equal shares, but you must not sell any part of the farm. I have a reason for this. What treasure I have lies within half an arm's length below the ground.'

The sons thought their father was talking about money he had buried. After the old man died, they dug up the whole farm. They found no buried treasure, but the ground was so well turned over that splendid crops grew. That was the treasure the old man spoke about.

Tick the box against each sentence that is true.

1 The farmer said all his wealth lay on the farm. ☐

2 What he said was true. ☐

3 He hid the money so nobody could find it. ☐

4 The sons were hoping to find money. ☐

5 Every part of the land was dug up. ☐

6 By digging so much they spoiled a crop. ☐

Anagrams 1

Write the missing word in each sentence. This word is made up of all the letters in the word printed in bold type. In the last sentence the first letter of the word is given to you.

1 Out **cat** will ______________ strangely if it hears a dog bark.

2 He had an **ache** in ________________ one of his ears.

3 At the zoo I watched **apes** eating fresh ___________ in pods.

4 The burglar went to **bury** the stolen _____________.

5 As sound began to **fade**, she thought she was ___________.

6 I'd like to **read** that book but it is too ____________ to buy.

7 **Mabel** took the_______________ for breaking the window.

8 I was told that the **Devil** ____________ down in a fiery world.

9 What was a **dingo**_______________ to be so close to town?

10 **Bertha** took a deep **b**__________

and blew out the candles.

What is a glacier?

A glacier is a river, but unlike an ordinary river, it is frozen. The glacier begins in high mountains of cold parts of the world that are covered with snow. More and more snow falls and is pushed down to make rivers of solid ice.

As the glaciers slowly flow down the mountain valleys, scratching and grinding the rocks, they carry stones and boulders. Most glaciers melt when they reach warmer climates. Some, near the North Pole, stay frozen until reaching the sea. Icy chunks break off into icebergs.

Thousands of years ago during the Ice Age, the world had many more glaciers. Today there are many deep valleys that were carved out by glaciers in the past. Now only a small river or stream flows through the rocky sides that were once gouged out by the slow moving ice.

Use a word from the story to fill each space.

1 Glaciers begin where there is ____________ on mountains.

2 Glaciers carry boulders and ________________ with them.

3 Icebergs form from glaciers near the North ______________.

4 What remain today that were made by very old glaciers? ______________

5 Which word means the same as **coated**? ________________

6 Which word means the opposite of **shallow**? ______________

Missing words 3

One word is missing in each line where there are four dots. Write the word that you think should be there.

The *Titanic* was one of the largest liners ever b.... . 1 ____________

Its f.... voyage was from England to America 2 ____________

in 1912. The huge ship h.... an iceberg at night. 3 ____________

There was no radar then. Lifeboats w.... 4 ____________

lowered when not yet f.... of people. 5 ____________

This left many on board. W.... flooded in. 6 ____________

As the bow went d...., the stern tilted up in 7 ____________

the air. Soon the s.... was gone below the 8 ____________

surface, taking over fifteen hundred m.... , 9 ____________

women and children to their d.... . 10 ____________

In 1985, a t.... submarine with no crew but 11 ____________

equipped with a television c.... sighted the 12 ____________

w.... . Two years later a special submarine 13 ____________

carrying three men l.... closely at the *Titanic*. 14 ____________

How does a snake move?

When a snake moves, it glides along the ground. Three parts of the snake's body work together to do this: the backbone, the ribs and the large horny scales underneath.

There is one rib for each part of the backbone, and each rib is fixed to a scale on the belly. The muscles on the ribs move the scales forward, one after the other. The snake's body then moves from side to side and glides along.

The movement of a snake is very like a boat that is being rowed on water. The ribs are like oars, but instead of gripping water, they grip the ground. A boat, of course, is rigid but a snake's body is flexible.

Use a word from the story to fill each space.

1 A snake moves when it ____________ along the ground.

2 To do this it uses scales, backbone and ________________.

3 A snake's body moves from side to ________________.

4 Snakes move like a rowing ______________ on water.

5 Which word means the same as **fastened**? ______________

6 Which word means the opposite of **backward**? ____________

Who made the rotary clothes hoist?

The Hills rotary hoist is a frame of metal with wires. It has four sides, and wet clothes are hung on the wires. The whole hoist can be raised or lowered by turning a handle. Old clotheslines for drying laundry were strung across the backyard. They needed long wooden props.

The man who invented this wonderful new way of drying clothes was Lance Hill. He was a motor mechanic from Adelaide, Australia. His backyard had a few trees that were growing fast. He was finding less and less room for his old clothesline. His first hoist was made from scraps of metal. Later, in his factory, Lance made all the parts with metal tubing. His rotary hoist was sold to countries in many parts of the world.

Use a word from the story to fill each space.

1 There are four sides to a rotary ______________.

2 Old clotheslines needed wooden ______________.

3 Lance Hill lived in the city of ______________.

4 Arms of hoists are now made of metal ______________.

5 Which word means the same as **bits**? ______________

6 Which word means the opposite of **wetting**? ______________

Change words 1

Use all the letters of the word in bold type to make a new word to match the clue. The first letter of the last five words is given to help you.

1 Change **pore** into something we use to tie things. __________

2 Change **deal** into a heavy metal. __________________

3 Change **kids** into a word meaning 'slide'. _______________

4 Change **seat** into a point of the compass. _______________

5 Change **loaf** into a young animal. _____________

6 Change **lump** into a fruit. ______________

7 Change **reed** into an animal. _________________

8 Change **peels** into something we do at night. **s**_____________

9 Change **horse** into land near the sea. **s**_________________

10 Change **trace** into a wooden box. **c**_________________

11 Change **lived** into a wicked person. **d**_________________

12 Change **liars** into something trains run on. **r**_______________

Respect the senior citizen

Years ago in Australia, an old hunting dog was out with two younger dogs and a farmer. They were after a wild pig that had been eating the crops. This dog was almost blind in one eye but was the first to seize a boar by its hind leg. However, the dog's old broken teeth were not able to hold tightly, and the male pig escaped.

The farmer flew into a rage and struck the poor old dog with a stick. He kept hitting the animal and saying how the dog was so useless.

The dog whimpered and said, 'Do not hit your old faithful dog. I am sorry about the boar, but think of all the pigs I helped you catch or kill. I may be old now but I tried my best.'

Tick the box against each sentence that is true.

1 The farmer and his dogs were hunting pigs. ☐

2 The three dogs were all old. ☐

3 One dog was unable to bite properly. ☐

4 The farmer was very angry with one dog. ☐

5 The farmer used a whip to punish the dog. ☐

6 The dog reminded the farmer that he had served him well. ☐

Where do we find gold?

Gold is a metal that is very scarce. Because it is scarce, it is expensive to buy. Rings and other jewellery are made of gold. For thousands of years people have been searching for this precious metal. Many early settlers came to Australia because they heard that gold could be found near Bathurst. This was called a 'gold rush'.

Rain, which forms streams and then rivers, washes metals from rocks. Fine grains or specks of gold are carried downhill. They can be found in sandy or muddy banks of some rivers. Sometimes big pieces of gold are washed down in lumps. We call them nuggets.

Gold is also found well below the ground. The yellow metal runs in seams through solid rock. Miners with special cutting tools cut through rock with veins of gold. The broken rock is trucked to the surface where it is treated and the gold is separated by special machinery.

Use a word from the story to fill each space.

1 Gold is an expensive ______________.

2 Rivers carry tiny grains or ________________ of gold.

3 Lumps of gold are called ________________.

4 A person who digs underground is a ______________.

5 Which word means the same as **under**? ______________

6 Which word means the opposite of **joined**? ____________

Which two words rhyme?

Read each group of three words. Two in each line rhyme. Write those two in the space.

1 waft raft loft ______________________

2 ghoul mule foul ______________________

3 guy flea ski ______________________

4 quaff rough cough ______________________

5 dove shove move ______________________

6 bury fury jury ______________________

7 worth death earth ______________________

8 nude should feud ______________________

9 plough dough toe ______________________

10 moth lathe wrath ______________________

11 plait hate spat ______________________

12 stone gone shone ______________________

Which animal cannot turn its head?

The crocodile can turn its whole body but cannot turn its head like most other animals. The reason is that it has a strange formation of neck bones. They are locked together. This has perhaps saved some lives when humans or animals have come close to a crocodile's snapping jaws.

On the other hand, it does not pay for either animal or human to come close to a crocodile's tail. It can swing round and knock anything off its feet with one powerful flick.

Crocodiles like catching victims in the water. Those they catch on land they will drag back into the water. Here they are helped by nature. They can tear a body to pieces without swallowing water. At the tip of its snout the crocodile has nostrils which are connected by a tube that goes right down its windpipe.

Use a word from the story to fill each space.

1 A crocodile is unable to turn its ________________.

2 A crocodile can ________________ its tail.

3 Crocodile victims are dragged back into ________________.

4 The windpipe of a crocodile is connected to its ______________.

5 Which word means the same as **odd**? ________________

6 Which word means the opposite of **separated**? ______________

What is a locust?

A locust is a kind of grasshopper. There are many kinds which vary in size from 10 millimetres to 10 centimetres in length. All have the habit of drilling holes in the earth in which to lay their many eggs. From the eggs come little locusts, like their parents but without wings until they have shed their skins several times.

Locusts are very hungry insects. They eat any green plant life within reach. When there is no food left, they rise up in a swarm and fly somewhere else to find another meal. Farmers hate locusts as they very often destroy whole crops. The best way to get rid of locusts is to poison the young locusts before they are able to fly.

Use a word from the story to fill each space.

1 A locust is really a ________________.

2 Grasshoppers drill holes in which to lay ________________.

3 Locusts eat ________________ plants.

4 Many locusts flying together make a ________________.

5 Which word means the same as **ground**? ________________

6 Which word means the opposite of **adore**? ________________

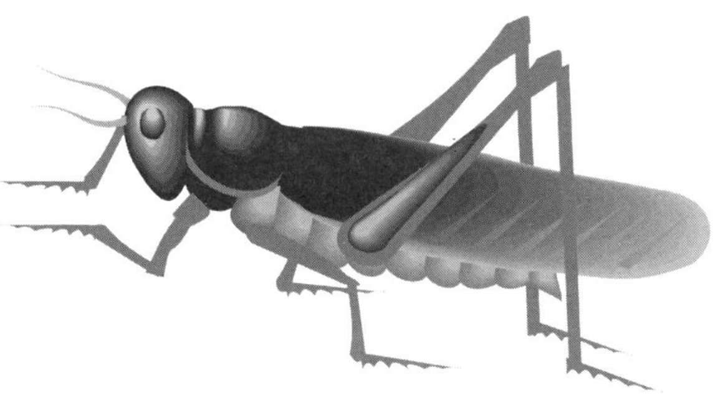

One word is not needed 1

Find the word in each sentence that could be left out. Write it in the space.

1 She ate a banana, an apple and also a peach. ____________

2 Where do you live at nowadays? ____________

3 I must return back home soon. ____________

4 We seldom ever go to the beach on Saturdays. ____________

5 She fell off of her bike yesterday morning. ____________

6 She taught swimming up until last week. ____________

7 The rain it continued to fall all day. ____________

8 Not long ago we recently saw a rare owl. ____________

9 The two cousins are both alike in looks. ____________

10 Mum has to renew her driving licence again. ____________

11 Follow behind me and I'll lead you home. ____________

12 The wet rain soaked my clothes yesterday. ____________

13 The three triplets were born at the hospital. ____________

Don't sneer at things you can't have

A hungry fox had been trying to break into a fowl yard to snatch a chicken or hen for his dinner. The farmer had built a very strong barbed wire fence to stop foxes from stealing.

The fox became hungrier and hungrier. He kept walking until he came to a vineyard where some fine grapes were growing. Unluckily for the fox, the ripe purple grapes were all growing on a long trellis. They were too high up for him to reach – even when he stood on his hind legs.

'Oh well, never mind,' said the fox to himself. 'Anyone else is welcome to those rotten grapes. I am sure they are sour anyway, and would have only given me a stomach ache.'

Tick the box against each sentence that is true.

1 The fox was after a baby goose for his dinner. ☐

2 A wooden fence had been built by the farmer. ☐

3 The grapes in the vineyard were ready for eating. ☐

4 The fox would have liked to eat the grapes. ☐

5 The grapes were out of reach for the fox. ☐

6 The grapes really were sour. ☐

Can a fly hear?

There are very few insects that can hear. Most of them, including flies, are deaf. Every kind of sound has been tried, but most insects take no notice at all. Scientists have even tried using sounds with a very high pitch. The pitch they used could not be heard by our ears. Still most insects took no notice.

Flies are not the only common insects that cannot hear. In another experiment, a violin string was scraped a centimetre away from bees that were busy taking pollen from flowers. They kept on working.

Although flies cannot hear, they can certainly see well. Each eye has hundreds of tiny mirror-like lenses. It is impossible to surprise a fly by creeping up to swat it. This nasty insect will spot your hand from whatever direction it comes – even if it comes from above.

Use a word from the story to fill each space.

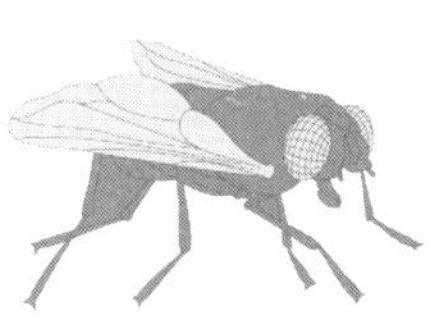

1 Most insects cannot ________________.

2 They take no notice of high ________________ sounds.

3 Which insect sees well? ________________

4 Which insects gather pollen? ________________

5 Which word means the same as **noises**? ________________

6 Which word means the opposite of **below**? ________________

Missing words 4

One word is missing in each line where there are four dots. Write the word that you think should be there.

The blue-ringed octopus is only a l....	1	______
larger t.... a man's hand. Normally it is	2	______
striped, with brown bands. I.... disturbed,	3	______
these b.... turn bright blue.	4	______
This octopus l.... in rocky pools all round	5	______
the coast of Australia. Be v.... careful	6	______
not to t.... or go near it. The little creature	7	______
b.... and injects a deadly poison. Unless	8	______
treated quickly, a victim will d.... .	9	______
This octopus is n.... vicious. Its poison	10	______
is used to catch f.... . It loves to eat crabs.	11	______
When a c.... comes near, the octopus	12	______
squirts p.... at it. The crab then drinks	13	______
the poison and can no l.... move away.	14	______

Where was the first snapshot taken?

In 1826 a man in France took the very first snapshot, or photograph. The likeness was formed on a metal plate covered with bitumen. Twelve years later another man improved on the idea. He was Jacques Daguerre. This time he used a copper plate coated with silver. When the camera clicked, light fell on the plate and a picture could be developed by using chemicals. Daguerre's camera was a huge box with a lens that poked out. This lens was focused by hand like a telescope.

In 1888 an American, George Eastman, developed a small camera. It could be easily held in the hand. It had a celluloid roll of film instead of a metal plate. By 1900 a simple little box camera called the 'Brownie' made by the Eastman Kodak company became popular. Better cameras with expensive lenses were made from 1920 to 1940 in Germany. Now most cameras are made in Japan.

Use a word from the story to fill each space.

1 The first photographic ____________ was coated with bitumen.

2 Jacques Daguerre coated a plate with ________________.

3 George ________________ invented a celluloid roll of film.

4 Which country today makes many cameras? ______________

5 Which word means the same as **costly**? ________________

6 Which word means the opposite of **tiny**? ________________

What is rubber?

Spanish explorers first saw rubber in South America. Natives played with solid rubber balls that bounced off the ground. It did not take the Spaniards long to discover that rubber was a kind of gum that oozed from trees. For many years traders brought rubber to Europe.

Some 200 years later it was found that little cubes of gum could be used for rubbing out pencil marks. In 1823 Charles Macintosh used rubber mixed with cloth to make waterproof raincoats. Other uses were found for rubber after it was treated with chemicals.

Then began the race to plant rubber trees. The best kind of rubber tree grew in Brazil. The Brazilians would not let anyone take seeds from Brazil. An Englishman smuggled seeds out and they were planted in Kew Gardens, London. The seeds grew well and small trees were sent to be planted in Malaya, a country owned by Britain. There, thousands of rubber trees grew in plantations.

Use a word from the story to fill each space.

1. Rubber is a kind of ___________________.
2. Cubes of rubber took out __________________ marks.
3. At first, the best rubber trees grew in ___________________.
4. To see Kew Gardens you must go to __________________.
5. Which word means the same as **find**? __________________
6. Which word means the opposite of **worst**? ________________

Answers

Page 1 Tick **1**, **3** and **4**

Page 2 **1** land **2** chasm **3** Philippines **4** supersonic **5** varies **6** exact

Page 3 **1** well **2** gang **3** money **4** police **5** fierce **6** men **7** iron **8** was **9** one **10** moved **11** wounded **12** hospital **13** guilty **14** death

Page 4 **1** dark **2** radar **3** fruit **4** vampire **5** cluster **6** suck

Page 5 **1** Vesuvius **2** Pompeii **3** streets **4** museum **5** giant **6** molten

Page 6 **1** keeper **2** magician **3** usher **4** pirate **5** police officer **6** burglar **7** barber **8** acrobat **9** violinist **10** groom

Page 7 Tick **2**, **5** and **6**

Page 8 **1** France **2** germs **3** heating **4** pasteurisation **5** found **6** sour

Page 9 **1** different **2** kinds **3** small **4** size **5** fish **6** made **7** like **8** shark **9** fat **10** watch **11** seal **12** larger **13** died **14** sea or seas

Page 10 **1** Liverpool **2** Starr **3** record **4** America **5** spotted **6** rich

Page 11 **1** detective **2** spy **3** jeweller **4** doorman **5** smuggler **6** optician **7** matador **8** builder **9** minister **10** ballerina

Page 12 **1** throttle **2** rudders **3** stalling **4** brakes **5** single **6** pull

Page 13 Tick **1**, **2**, **4** and **5**

Page 14 **1** act **2** each **3** peas **4** ruby **5** deaf **6** dear **7** blame **8** lived **9** doing **10** breath

Page 15 **1** snow **2** stones **3** Pole **4** valleys **5** covered **6** deep

Page 16 **1** built **2** first **3** hit **4** were **5** full **6** water **7** down **8** ship **9** men **10** death or deaths **11** tiny **12** camera **13** wreck **14** looked

Page 17 **1** glides **2** ribs **3** side **4** boat **5** fixed **6** forward

Page 18 **1** hoist **2** props **3** Adelaide **4** tubing **5** scraps **6** drying

Page 19 **1** rope **2** lead **3** skid **4** east **5** foal **6** plum **7** deer **8** sleep **9** shore **10** crate **11** devil **12** rails

Page 20 Tick **1**, **3**, **4** and **6**

Page 21 **1** metal **2** specks **3** nuggets **4** miner **5** below **6** separated

Page 22 **1** waft loft **2** ghoul mule **3** flea ski **4** quaff cough **5** dove shove **6** fury jury **7** worth earth **8** nude feud **9** dough toe **10** moth wrath **11** plait spat **12** gone shone

Page 23 **1** head **2** flick **3** water **4** nostrils **5** strange **6** connected

Page 24 **1** grasshopper **2** eggs **3** green **4** swarm **5** earth **6** hate

Page 25 **1** also **2** at **3** back **4** ever **5** of **6** up **7** it **8** recently **9** both **10** again **11** behind **12** wet **13** three

Page 26 Tick **3**, **4** and **5**

Page 27 **1** hear **2** pitch **3** fly **4** bees **5** sounds **6** above

Page 28 **1** little **2** than **3** if **4** bands **5** lives **6** very **7** touch **8** bites **9** die **10** not **11** food **12** crab **13** poison **14** longer

Page 29 **1** plate **2** silver **3** Eastman **4** Japan **5** expensive **6** huge

Page 30 **1** gum **2** pencil **3** Brazil **4** London **5** discover **6** best

Page 31 **1** soldier **2** palmist **3** engineer **4** warder **5** milliner **6** landlord **7** painter **8** beekeeper **9** inventor **10** printer

Page 32 Tick **3**, **4**, **5** and **6**

Page 33 **1** musicians **2** flavouring **3** containers **4** footwear **5** livestock **6** smell **7** bedding **8** utensils **9** weapons **10** metal **11** vehicles **12** snakes

Page 34 **1** clay **2** Iraq **3** wood **4** spokes **5** someone **6** simple

Page 35 **1** soft **2** thread **3** England **4** China **5** cloth **6** sold

Page 36 **1** fir **2** prise **3** hangar **4** canvas **5** cache **6** vein **7** minor **8** lightning **9** story **10** links **11** cereal **12** birth

Page 37 **1** America **2** Wrigley **3** chicle **4** machines **5** lump **6** refused

Page 38 Tick **3**, **4** and **5**

Page 39 **1** kept **2** day **3** long **4** inn **5** live **6** arrived **7** wore **8** very **9** sang **10** sing **11** later **12** men **13** bottle

Page 40 **1** night **2** skins **3** books **4** bones **5** pieces **6** found

Page 41 **1** hear **2** hips **3** elbow **4** dines **5** canoe **6** later **7** lives **8** ladies **9** hornet **10** warden

Page 42 **1** dots **2** finger **3** France **4** library **5** cluster **6** borrow

Page 43 **1** fish **2** bone **3** pups **4** gills **5** baby **6** alive

Page 44 **1** teller **2** forger **3** gymnast **4** maid **5** matron **6** scout **7** organist **8** caddy **9** grazier **10** sculptor

Page 45 Tick **1**, **2** and **5**

Page 46 **1** female **2** mane **3** zebra **4** young **5** bushy **6** strong

Page 47 **1** time **2** send **3** who **4** said **5** were **6** with **7** ships **8** left **9** year **10** began **11** and **12** buildings **13** food **14** capital

Page 48 **1** male **2** Sydney **3** antidote **4** rock **5** venom **6** entrance

Page 49 **1** wolf **2** last **3** star **4** spear **5** cried **6** table **7** teach **8** outer **9** snake **10** broad **11** lobster **12** dance

Page 50 **1** salt **2** sea **3** clouds **4** boiling **5** stays **6** fresh

Page 51 Tick **3**, **4**, **5** and **6**

Page 52 **1** kinds **2** spider **3** size **4** also **5** name **6** sound **7** birds **8** eat **9** was **10** ill **11** died **12** dog **13** lives **14** hot

Page 53 **1** America **2** fifteen **3** five **4** Benz **5** sold **6** wealthiest

Page 54 **1** beaks **2** water **3** fish **4** planes **5** terrified **6** awkward

Page 55 **1** pears **2** armed **3** chain **4** dishes **5** cellar **6** resign **7** pistol **8** kippers **9** repaint **10** erupted

Page 56 **1** flint **2** woodpecker **3** branches **4** baboon **5** copy **6** enjoy

Page 57 Tick **3**, **4** and **5**

Page 58 **1** novelist **2** diver **3** chemist **4** medallist **5** angler **6** gladiator **7** bookmaker **8** model **9** florist **10** settler

Page 59 **1** die **2** cross **3** Geneva **4** hospital **5** protect **6** best

Page 60 **1** cooked **2** germs **3** boiled **4** raw **5** lump **6** ill

Page 61 **1** like **2** shines **3** fields **4** trees **5** mouse **6** door **7** lies **8** moon **9** day **10** sleep **11** eyes **12** sun

Page 62 **1** axle **2** rubbing **3** bearings **4** ground **5** slip **6** still

Page 63 Tick **1**, **5** and **6**

Page 64 **1** after **2** round **3** old **4** unknown **5** together **6** to **7** two **8** it **9** got **10** down **11** again **12** up

Who is speaking? 3

Read each sentence. Write who is speaking in the space. Choose answers from the box.

engineer	**beekeeper**	**soldier**	**inventor**	**palmist**
printer	**landlord**	**warder**	**milliner**	**painter**

1 I will need more ammunition soon. ______________

2 You are going to be famous one day. ______________

3 Drawings for the bridge footings are ready. ______________

4 All the prisoners must stay in their cells today. ______________

5 This is our latest style of hats. ______________

6 You are two months behind in the rent. ______________

7 My watercolours and oils sell well these days. ______________

8 I had better go and check the hives. ______________

9 It has taken two years to perfect this gadget. ______________

10 The first copies are due off the press today. ______________

What goes around, comes around

A horse and a donkey were travelling along a road together with the man who owned them. The horse had nothing on his back, but the poor donkey was so heavily laden that he could hardly keep moving. He begged the horse to help him.

The horse was bad-tempered and only thought about himself. He refused. Shortly afterwards the donkey fell exhausted on the road and died. The owner took the whole load that the donkey was carrying and placed it on the horse's back. On top of that he decided to ride on the horse himself.

Now it was the horse's turn to be struggling with an even heavier load than the donkey was carrying. The horse, by not thinking of how the donkey felt, brought upon himself a great deal of work and trouble.

Tick the box against each sentence that is true.

1 The horse and the donkey were pulling a cart. ☐

2 At first the horse carried part of the load. ☐

3 The weight of the load caused the donkey to die. ☐

4 The horse only thought of his own feelings. ☐

5 The owner was unfair in the first place. ☐

6 The horse would have been better off doing his fair share. ☐

Which word names the group?

In each line of words one of them names the other three. Write this group word in the space.

1 violinists musicians pianists drummers ________________

2 mint chocolate vanilla flavouring ________________

3 cans jars containers flagons ________________

4 wellingtons footwear sandals thongs ________________

5 pigs cattle sheep livestock ________________

6 pungent musty smell scented ________________

7 sheets bedding blankets quilts ________________

8 utensils pots pans colanders ________________

9 swords weapons daggers rifles ________________

10 copper iron steel metal ________________

11 buses vehicles trucks vans ________________

12 vipers adders cobras snakes ________________

Where were wheels first used?

The wheel is such a clever invention. It is used in cars, bikes, clocks and most machines. Before anyone thought of a wheel, everything was dragged along the ground.

The wheel was first used by men and women who made pots out of clay for carrying water. This was over five thousand years ago in Iraq. Even today, a potter uses a spinning wheel to make clay pots, cups and plates.

Soon after, someone thought of using wheels to help move things. At first, solid wheels cut from wood were made and used in a simple cart. The cart was pulled along by oxen.

After another 1500 years wheels were made with spokes. These were lighter and used for chariots. It was not long before all wheels of carts and coaches had spokes.

Use a word from the story to fill each space.

1 The first wheel was used to make

__________________ pots.

2 In which country was the wheel

invented? ________________

3 The first cart wheels were cut from solid __________________.

4 Wheels with _________________ were lighter than solid ones.

5 Which word means the same as **somebody**? _______________

6 Which word means the opposite of **complicated**? __________

How were the first clothes made?

People long ago made their clothes from animal skins. The animal was killed and the skin was pegged out to dry. To make the skin soft, it was hammered with stones, then cut into shape and sewn together.

The next big step in making clothes came when people learnt to make cloth. Cotton, wool, flax or hemp was spun to make a thin thread. The thread was woven on a loom to make cloth. Later, about 700 years ago, a loom with foot pedals was first used to weave cloth.

Then about 260 years ago mechanical looms were invented in England. They were driven by steam, and cloth for clothes could be made quickly in factories. England sold clothes all over the world.

Today China has the latest spinning and weaving machines and many factories. It now sells a lot of clothes to other countries.

Use a word from the story to fill each space.

1 Before sewing, animal skins had to be dried and made ________________.

2 Cotton has to be spun into a thin ________________.

3 In which country were mechanical looms invented? ____________

4 Which country today sells a lot of clothes? ______________.

5 Which word means the same as **material**? ________________

6 Which word means the opposite of **bought**? ______________

Same sounding words

In each sentence two words are printed in bold type. Decide which one is correct. Write this word in the space.

1 Parrots roost in that **fir fur** tree. ______________

2 The thief tried to **prise prize** open the safe. ______________

3 Planes are kept in a **hanger hangar**. ______________

4 Tents are made out of **canvas canvass**. ______________

5 The pirates found a **cash cache** of silver. ______________

6 The **vain vein** in my arm carries blood. ______________

7 There is only a **minor miner** dent in the car. ______________

8 I saw **lightning lightening** during the storm. ______________

9 She read me a **storey story** last night. ______________

10 Dad is out on the golf **links lynx** with his friend. ______________

11 For breakfast I always eat **cereal serial**. ______________

12 My aunt gave **birth berth** to a healthy boy. ______________

What is chewing gum?

In America, a man named Adam Smith was making things from rubber in his factory. He had a small lump of chicle, which is the sap from a rubbery gum tree. For fun, he popped it into his mouth. He chewed and chewed on the chicle but it stayed whole.

Adam had a bright idea. Why not heat up the chicle and add a mint flavour? He could then sell the chicle and call it chewing gum.

In 1872 Adam opened a small factory. Shopkeepers refused to sell the chewing gum, so the Tutti-Frutti company sold it in slot machines. You could buy chewing gum at railway stations.

A company in England called Wrigley started selling this chewing gum from machines in 1911. It became popular there, and Wrigley's chewing gum was soon selling to many countries, including Australia. It is still sold and chewed all over the world.

Use a word from the story to fill each space.

1 In which country was chewing gum first made? ____________

2 The English company that sells chewing gum is ____________.

3 Chewing gum is made from a sap called ____________.

4 Tutti-Frutti sold chewing gum from slot ____________.

5 Which word means the same as **piece**? ____________

6 Which word means the opposite of **agreed**? ____________

Flattery is not always sincere

A hungry fox was wandering through the forest. He glanced up and noticed a crow sitting on a tree branch. In its mouth, the crow had a piece of cheese. 'My oh my, you are the prettiest crow I have ever seen,' said the fox. 'I only wish you would sing a song for me. A bird with lovely feathers always has a sweet voice, and it is such a long time since I heard any fine music. Come on, be a good bird and make a poor old fox happy.'

The silly crow puffed out its feathers. It felt so proud at being asked to sing. The bird could not help itself. It opened its mouth to caw and let the piece of cheese fall to the ground.

The cunning fox snapped it up and said to himself as he trotted away: 'I said she was beautiful, but I never said she was clever.'

Tick the box against each sentence that is true.

1 The crow had stolen the cheese from the fox. ☐

2 The fox had been following the crow. ☐

3 The fox just happened to see the crow with the cheese. ☐

4 The crow was flattered by what the fox said. ☐

5 The crow stupidly fell for the fox's trick. ☐

6 The loser was the fox. ☐

Missing words 5

One word is missing in each line where there are four dots. Write the word that you think should be there. This page is adapted from *Treasure Island* by R. L. Stevenson.

My father k.... an inn by the sea called the	1	____________
Admiral Benbow. I clearly remember the d....	2	____________
when the old brown seaman, with the l.... white	3	____________
scar down his cheek, walked into the i.... . He	4	____________
came to l.... with us there.	5	____________
The day he a...., he brought his sea-chest and	6	____________
I remember he w.... a dirty blue coat. His	7	____________
hands were v.... dirty and rough, and his nails	8	____________
quite black. He looked out to the bay, then s....	9	____________
that old sea song he was to s.... so often	10	____________
l.... on.	11	____________
'Fifteen m.... on a dead man's chest	12	____________
Yo-ho-ho and a b.... of rum!'	13	____________

Where are the oldest drawings?

Long ago people had no houses. They lived in caves that were once homes to wild animals. At night men and women built fires near the entrance to frighten animals that might come looking for shelter. During the day a group of men would go hunting animals. They killed them for meat, and the women made clothes from their skins.

On the walls of old caves, drawings and carvings have been found. There are pictures of bears, wild pigs and deer. Photos of them can be found in books. These people even drew and carved animals on pieces of bones or stones. We keep them in special museums so we can still see them today.

Cave people made knives with handles cleverly carved out of bones. They also made ornaments from animal horns and teeth.

Use a word from the story to fill each space.

1 Fires at ________________ kept wild animals away.

2 Cave men and women used animal ________ to make clothes.

3 Photos of old drawings can be seen in ________________.

4 Sometimes drawings were made on stones or pieces of

________________.

5 Which word means the same as **bits**? ________________

6 Which word means the opposite of **lost**? ________________

Anagrams 2

Write the missing word in each sentence. This word is made up of all the letters in the word printed in bold type. In the last three sentences the first letter of the word is given to you.

1 A **hare** can ______________ well as it has long ears.

2 Mary slipped on the deck of a **ship** and hurt her ___________.

3 The bullet entered just **below** his ____________.

4 **Denis** ______________ on seafood twice a week.

5 The islanders first crossed the **ocean** by _____________.

6 Mum said she would **alter** my skirt _____________ tonight.

7 Women in that country wear **veils** all their _______________.

8 The boat **sailed** with the men, leaving the **l**_________ behind.

9 Sitting on his **throne**, the king was stung by a

h____________.

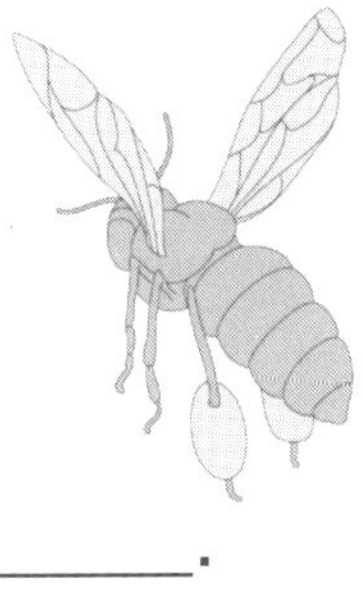

10 **Andrew** was the name of the prison **w**_____________.

How can a blind person read?

A blind person cannot read ordinary books because he or she cannot see the letters. All this changed when a Frenchman, Louis Braille, invented a system of raised dots. Each letter was represented by a different pattern of dots. The dots felt like a small cluster of pin heads when touched with the tip of a finger.

Just over a hundred years ago, the first book with raised dots was printed in France. Now thousands of these books are printed in many countries all over the world. The style of Braille has been changed slightly and is now known as Standard English Braille.

Anyone who is blind can go to a library and borrow a book. When blind people learn to read, they learn the special Braille alphabet. It is wonderful that blind people can share the enjoyment and knowledge that comes from books.

Use a word from the story to fill each space.

1 Braille's system was made up of raised ____________________.

2 To read Braille a person uses a ____________________.

3 The first Braille book was made in ____________________.

4 We can borrow a Braille book from the ____________________.

5 Which word means the same as **group**? ____________________

6 Which word means the opposite of **lend**? ____________________

Why are sharks different?

There are hundreds of kinds of sharks. They all belong to the large family of fish that live in the sea, but fish and sharks are different in many ways.

The skeleton of a fish is made of bones. The skeleton of a shark is made of cartilage. Cartilage can be bent and is like rubber. You can bend you ears because they are made of cartilage.

Fish lay eggs in the sea and baby fish hatch out of the eggs. Most sharks give birth to babies that are alive. We call them pups.

All fish have gills. Water passes in and out of these gills. Oxygen is taken from the water just as we take oxygen from the air we breathe.

Most fish have one set of gills, or opening, on each side of the head. A shark has five openings on each side. If you are fishing and catch a baby shark, it will be easily recognised.

Use a word from the story to fill each space.

1 Sharks belong to the ________________ family.

2 Sharks do not have a skeleton made of ________________.

3 Young sharks are called ________________.

4 A fish breathes through its ________________.

5 Which word means the same as **young**? ________________

6 Which word means the opposite of **dead**? ________________

Who is speaking? 4

Read each sentence. Write who is speaking in the space. Choose answers from the box.

gymnast	**maid**	**caddy**	**forger**	**organist**
scout	**grazier**	**sculptor**	**matron**	**teller**

1. Would you like it in 50 or 100 dollar notes? ________________
2. Nobody will know this is not his signature. ________________
3. I must work out on the parallel bars. ____________________
4. Should I change the sheets today, madam? ______________
5. Keep checking his blood pressure, nurse. _________________
6. Our troop is going camping for four days. _________________
7. The family wants me to play something lively. _____________
8. I suggest you use a number four iron. ___________________
9. We will be short of grass if it doesn't rain soon. ___________
10. I have nearly finished this bronze bust. __________________

Bad company leads to trouble

A farmer grew corn but had trouble with thieves. Wild cranes and geese would fly into his fields and eat the newly sown corn seeds before they had time to grow.

The farmer made a string net which fell over birds if they tripped a fine cotton cord. One day several of these birds were caught when the net collapsed on top of them.

Among the birds was a stork who pleaded for his life. 'I did not come here to steal corn,' he said. 'I only came to keep these birds company. They are my friends.'

'What you say may or may not be true,' replied the farmer. 'But as I have caught you with the thieves, I will treat you as a thief. You must suffer the same fate as them.'

Tick the box against each sentence that is true.

1 The farmer knew his corn was being stolen. ☐

2 The farmer was sure that among the thieves were geese. ☐

3 The farmer made a trap entirely of cotton. ☐

4 Among the thieves was a crow. ☐

5 A stork said he was not there to steal. ☐

6 The farmer felt sorry for the stork. ☐

Which lions go hunting?

Lions live together in a group called a pride. There is always one or more male lions in the pride. They guard the pride against other lions or beasts. The rest are females or cubs.

The male lion is larger and stronger than the female. He has a bushy mane which makes him look even larger. This mane protects his neck when he fights other males. The strange thing about male lions in the pride is they do not go hunting for food. It is the females who go hunting together. They work as a team. They sometimes hunt at night if the moon is shining. Their favourite meals are zebra, wild pig or antelope.

The only male lions that go hunting are the young ones who leave the pride. Older lions force them out of the pride. These young males form a group of their own until they are strong enough to fight their way into a pride.

Use a word from the story to fill each space.

1 There are male and ________________ lions in a pride.

2 The male lion has a bushy ______________.

3 A pig, antelope or ________________ is part of a lion's diet.

4 ________________ male lions are forced out of the pride.

5 Which word means the same as **fluffy**? ______________

6 Which word means the opposite of **weak**? ______________

Missing words 6

One word is missing in each line where there are four dots. Write the word that you think should be there.

At one t.... in England, when jails were full, 1 ________________

it was decided to s.... convicts to Australia. 2 ________________

Joseph Banks, w.... had sailed with Captain 3 ________________

Cook, s.... it was a fine place to start a colony. 4 ________________

Eleven ships w.... made ready. Arthur Phillip 5 ________________

was in charge of 750 convicts, w.... 500 6 ________________

soldiers to guard them on the s.... . 7 ________________

The fleet l..... in May 1787. It did not arrive 8 ________________

until January the next y.... . 9 ________________

Work b.... on building a town. It was called 10 ________________

Port Jackson a.... later named Sydney. Houses, 11 ________________

office b.... and roads were built. Land was 12 ________________

prepared to grow f.... for convicts and soldiers. 13 ________________

So began what was to become the c.... of 14 ________________

New South Wales.

Which is the deadliest spider?

Most people agree that the world's deadliest spider is the Sydney funnel-web. It lives in the suburbs and surrounding country areas. The venom of the female is less harmful than that of the male. Bites from both spiders are painful, as the poison spreads quickly.

If you are bitten, a bandage should be applied over the wound. Do not try to cut off the blood supply. The next step is to call an ambulance or head to the nearest hospital. There you will be given an antidote which should save your life.

The web of the funnel-web does not look like a funnel but is more like a flat, silky, bag-like chamber. It is usually on the ground under a rock or log. Strung from the web there may be one or two entrance tunnels. These are connected by threads laid for the unsuspecting prey to bump into.

Use a word from the story to fill each space.

1 Venom of the ________________ is more harmful than that of the female.

2 Deadly spiders are found in and around the city of __________.

3 To attack the poison an ________________ is used.

4 Funnel-web spiders may hide under a log or ______________.

5 Which word means the same as **poison**? ________________

6 Which word means the opposite of **exit**? ________________

Change words 2

Use all the letters of the word in **bold type** to make a new word to match the clue. The first letter of the last nine words is given to help you.

1. Change **flow** into a wild animal. ________________
2. Change **salt** into the opposite of 'first'. ________________
3. Change **rats** into a bright object in the sky. ________________
4. Change **pears** into an ancient weapon. **s**________________
5. Change **cider** into something a baby has done. **c**________________
6. Change **bleat** into a piece of furniture. **t**________________
7. Change **cheat** into what teachers do. **t**________________
8. Change **route** into the opposite of 'inner'. **o**________________
9. Change **sneak** into a reptile. **s**________________
10. Change **board** into a word meaning 'wide'. **b**________________
11. Change **bolster** into an expensive seafood. **l**________________
12. Change **caned** into what ballet performers do. **d**________________

Why is the sea salty?

Sea water tastes salty because it contains lots of salt. It is the same kind of salt that we put on our food. This salt is found in rocks and soil on land. When it rains, tiny bits of salt are washed into rivers, which run into the sea.

The sun shines on the sea and water is sucked up to form clouds. Clouds bring rain over land but the water from clouds does not contain salt. This means more and more salt stays in the sea. No wonder the sea is so salty as this has been going on for millions of years.

We can make fresh water out of sea water. It is done by boiling salty water and collecting the steam. The steam is cooled and we have pure water to drink. Most large ships make their own fresh water.

Use a word from the story to fill each space.

1 Sea water has lots of __________________ in it.

2 Rivers run into the _________________.

3 The sun makes __________________ which carry rain.

4 By _______________ salt water we can collect fresh steam.

5 Which word means the same as **remains**? _________________

6 Which word means the opposite of **stale**? _________________

Talk doesn't get the job done

A fox was unlucky enough to fall down a well. He was swimming around in water which was about a metre from the top. The poor animal was becoming very tired and was in danger of drowning. After calling for help, he was pleased when a wolf arrived on the scene to see what was the matter.

'Oh, Mr Wolf,' cried the fox. 'Please lend me a paw and help me out, or I shall be drowned.'

'Poor thing,' cried the wolf. 'How sorry I am to see you in such a fix. How long have you been here? How ever did it happen? Is the well very deep?'

'Come on! This is no time for talking. Help me out of the water first, and then I will answer all the questions you wish to ask.'

Tick the box against each sentence that is true.

1 The fox went for a swim in the well. ☐

2 The fox was not in danger in the well. ☐

3 The wolf arrived when he heard cries for help. ☐

4 The wolf seemed sorry for the fox. ☐

5 The wolf did nothing but ask questions. ☐

6 We are not told whether the fox was finally rescued. ☐

Missing words 7

One word is missing in each line where there are four dots. Write the word that you think should be there to the right.

Australia is home to all k.... of spiders. The 1 ____________

largest is the bird-eating s.... . This hairy 2 ____________

creature is the s.... of a saucer and moves 3 ____________

very fast. It is a.... often called the barking 4 ____________

or whistling spider. This n.... is given to it 5 ____________

because of the peculiar grumbling s.... it 6 ____________

makes. Besides killing b...., this spider will 7 ____________

happily e.... the largest of frogs. 8 ____________

A woman was in the news lately when she w.... 9 ____________

bitten and became very i.... for several hours. 10 ____________

In another piece of news, a dog d.... soon 11 ____________

after it was bitten. The d.... was just being 12 ____________

curious.

Luckily for us, this spider l.... only in the state 13 ____________

of Queensland as it enjoys the h.... climate. 14 ____________

Who was Henry Ford?

You may have had a ride in a Ford motor car. If you haven't, then you must have seen one parked on the side of a road. Ford is a very famous name.

It was Henry Ford who was the first man to make cheap cars in very large numbers. The first car makers, Benz and Daimler, made cars slowly and carefully. They cost a lot of money.

Henry Ford was an American. His Ford cars were built in large factories. All the parts, including engines, wheels and seats, were put together by teams of workers.

In 1908, the first Ford Model T was made. Over fifteen million were sold. Workers in a Ford factory were paid well. They earned five dollars a day, which was a lot of money in those days. Henry became one of the wealthiest men in America. Today, Ford cars are made in many countries.

Use a word from the story to fill each space.

1 In which country were Ford cars first made? ______________

2 About how many million Model T cars were sold? ___________

3 How many dollars a day was a Ford worker paid? ___________

4 Which other make of car besides Ford and Daimler is mentioned in the text? ______________

5 Which word means the same as **marketed**? _______________

6 Which word means the same as **poorest**? _______________

Which sea birds fish together?

Pelicans look noble when you see them from a distance. Close up, they are quite funny to watch. They have an awkward way of walking, and their beaks are strange. The lower half is like a flexible bag. The upper part acts as a lid.

Pelicans can work as a team when they fish for a meal. These large birds form a half circle as they paddle together in the water. Each bird stays about a metre away from the next. They all swim from deep water into the shallows, driving the terrified shoals of fish before them. Then, when escape is impossible, the birds lower their great net-like bills and gobble up as many fish as possible.

The pelicans then waddle ashore, rest a while to digest their meal and leave. They either all paddle away in a group or take off like huge lumbering aeroplanes. After circling the area, they then fly off to another feeding area.

Use a word from the story to fill each space.

1 What parts of pelicans are strange? ____________________

2 The birds form a team when they are in the ____________________.

3 The main meal for a pelican is ____________________.

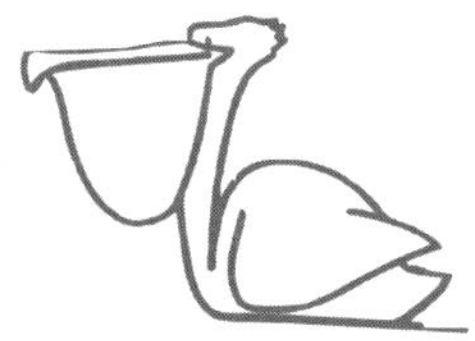

4 When flying, pelicans resemble jet ____________________.

5 Which word means the same as **frightened**? ____________________

6 Which word means the opposite of **graceful**? ____________________

Anagrams 3

Write the missing word in each sentence. This word is made up of all the letters in the word printed in bold type. One or more letters of the new word is given to you.

1 He asked the farmer if he could **spare** any **p**______________.

2 In my **dream** I was stopped by an **a**____________ robber.

3 This rare bird is from a **c**_____________ of mountains in **China**.

4 A snake **hissed** by her feet as she washed the **d**_____________.

5 I don't **recall** anyone hiding in my wine **c**_______________.

6 The **singer** was so ill that she was forced to **r**______________.

7 **Pilots** carry a **p**_________________ to fight any terrorist.

8 The **skipper** ordered **ki**___________ for breakfast that morning.

9 Dad hired a **painter** to **re**_____________ all the inside walls.

10 The volcano is **reputed** to have **er**___________ at one time.

Do animals use tools?

When we think of tools we imagine that they are something only used by humans. We know that early humans made tools. They chipped away at flint stones to make sharp knives. Hammers and spearheads were also made from stone, and needles were carved from bone.

Perhaps animals used objects as tools before early humans. We know they use them today. One bird, a kind of woodpecker, uses a cactus pine needle. It holds it in its beak and pokes into holes in trees, hoping to dig out grubs. Chimpanzees break off small branches from trees. They strip the bark and poke the thin end into ants' nests. These apes enjoy eating the young ant larvae they pull out of the nest.

Baboons pick up rocks to crack nuts. A recent television programme showed a young baboon trying to copy its mother. In the baby's hand was a stone, and it was trying to open a nut.

Use a word from the story to fill each space.

1 A type of stone used by early men and women was __________.

2 What kind of bird uses a pine needle? __________

3 Chimpanzees use tree __________ to poke out ants.

4 A monkey that breaks nuts with stones is a __________.

5 Which word means the same as **imitate**? __________

6 Which word means the opposite of **hate**? __________

Don't try to be too important

A bull, grazing in a field, near a pond, happened to put his foot down on a family of young frogs. One of them was crushed to death. The young frogs that lived to tell the tale explained to their mother that the bull was the biggest creature they had ever seen.

'Was it as big as this?' said the old frog, puffing herself up.

'Oh, much bigger than that!' cried the little frogs.

'As big as this?' she asked, straining herself even more.

'Indeed, Mother,' they said, 'you would never be so big even if you stretched until you burst.'

Then the foolish frog made another effort to make herself still bigger. She stretched herself so big that she burst and died.

Tick the box against each sentence that is true.

1 The bull killed two baby frogs. ☐

2 The bull sat on the frogs. ☐

3 The young frogs that lived told their mother. ☐

4 The mother wanted to know the size of the bull. ☐

5 She kept on making herself larger until she burst. ☐

6 The mother frog was not hurt badly. ☐

Who is speaking? 5

Read each sentence. Write who is speaking in the space. Choose answers from the box.

medallist	**bookmaker**	**model**	**settler**	**chemist**
florist	**gladiator**	**novelist**	**angler**	**diver**

1 This has been the hardest of my books to write. ____________

2 I was told to search for mines in the harbour. ____________

3 Your prescription is ready. ____________

4 I am so thrilled to have won gold. ____________

5 The fish were really biting today. ____________

6 One of us will die, and it better not be me. ____________

7 I'll give you ten to one if you bet on Lucky Lady. ____________

8 The dress is smart and comfortable. ____________

9 I suggest some roses and carnations. ____________

10 I never regret coming to live in Australia. ____________

What is the Red Cross?

Many soldiers are killed in battle. Some who are hit by bullets or shells do not die. They are wounded. Other soldiers who wear a red cross on their arm help them to an ambulance, which has a red cross painted on each side. The wounded end up in a hospital that has a red cross painted on the roof. This red cross is a sign that there are doctors and nurses helping wounded soldiers.

Nobody is allowed to shoot or bomb people or places that show or fly the red cross. This rule was agreed upon in 1861 when many countries met in Geneva, a city in Switzerland – the Swiss flag is a white cross on a red background. They decided that a red cross on a white background was the best flag to protect injured people. Hospital ships are painted white with a red cross clearly showing. This alerts submarines with torpedoes not to fire on them.

Use a word from the story to fill each space.

1 A soldier who is wounded may not ______________.

2 A hospital has a red ________________ painted on it.

3 The rule protecting the wounded was made in the city of

________________.

4 Submarines must not torpedo a ________________ ship.

5 Which word means the same as **guard**? ________________

6 Which word means the opposite of **worst**? ________________

Why do we cook food?

We cook food for many reasons. The best reason is that cooked food is easier to chew. Another good reason is that the cooking kills germs that might not be good for us.

Long ago a Frenchman, Louis Pasteur, found that there were germs in milk and these made people ill. Thanks to him, milk is now always boiled before it is sold to us in bottles or cartons.

Perhaps another good reason for cooking food is that it often looks better than raw food. Have you been to a butcher's shop? If you have, you must have seen plenty of raw meat. Sometimes there are traces of blood on the meat. How would you like to sit down for lunch or dinner and see a lump of raw meat on your plate? Or, worse still, how would you like to put a spoon into a runny raw egg and take a mouthful?

Use a word from the story to fill each space.

1 It is harder to chew food that is not ________________.

2 Food often has ________________ that are bad for us.

3 Milk we drink has already been ________________.

4 Meat that has not been cooked is ________________.

5 Which word means the same as **hunk**? ________________

6 Which word means the opposite of **healthy**? ________________

Missing words 8

One word is missing in each line where there are four dots. Write the word that you think should be there.

The moon has a face li.... the clock in the hall; 1 ______
She shi.... on thieves on the garden wall, 2 ______
On streets and fie.... and harbour quays, 3 ______
And birdies asleep in the forks of tr.... . 4 ______
The squalling cat and the squeaking mo...., 5 ______
The howling dog by the do.... of the house, 6 ______
The bat that li.... in bed at noon, 7 ______
All love to be out by the light of the mo.... . 8 ______
But of all the things that belong to the d.... 9 ______
Cuddle to sle.... to be out of her way; 10 ______
And flowers and children close their ey.... . 11 ______
Till up in the morning the su.... shall arise. 12 ______

Robert Louis Stevenson (1850–1894)

Why does oil help wheels turn?

Oil on the road will make a wheel slip. The oil will stop the wheel from gripping. However, there is an important place that needs oiling to help a wheel turn easily. This is where a wheel turns on an axle. The axle remains still, but the wheel spins. The oil or grease forms a smooth layer between the wheel and axle. This prevents two metals rubbing together and wearing.
An even better way of avoiding wear is to use little steel balls, with a light coating of oil. They are called ball bearings and look like steel marbles. The ball bearings are in a case surrounding the axle.

Oil is found deep under the ground. It is pumped up at oil wells. It is used as lubricating oil or grease, or it is refined to make petrol. There are so many cars and machines using oil that one day there will be little or no oil left.

Use a word from the story to fill each space.

1 Oil will help a wheel turn on its ______________.

2 Without oil, two metals would be ______________ together.

3 Small steel marbles are called ball ______________.

4 To find oil, people dig under the ______________.

5 Which word means the same as **slide**? ______________

6 Which word means the opposite of **moving**?

____

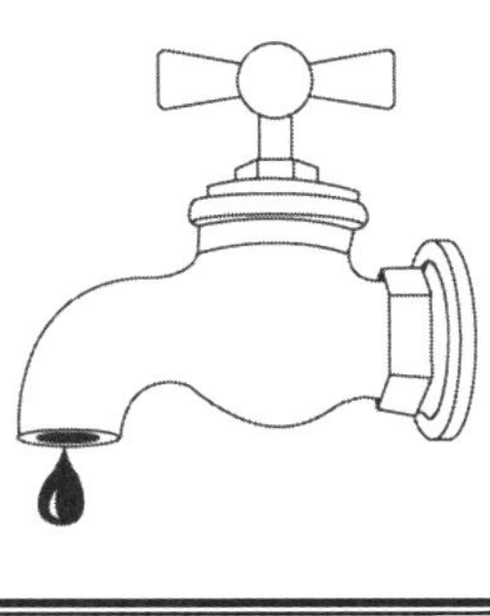

Beware of strangers

A mother goat, who was going out to search for food, locked her baby kid in the house. She warned him not to open the front door to anyone until she came back.

A wolf was hiding behind a bush close by and heard what she said. As soon as the mother had gone, he came and knocked at the front door. He imitated the mother goat and asked to be let into the house.

The kid happened to be looking through the keyhole. He could see that it was not his mother. In fact, the person knocking on the door looked strange. It had whiskers, and when it talked, it showed a set of very sharp teeth.

'No,' the kid shouted to the wolf. 'You aren't my mother or even an aunt. You are a stranger to me. In fact, you look like a picture of a wolf I once saw.'

Tick the box against each sentence that is true.

1 Mother goat went away and left a kid at home. ☐

2 A wolf was waiting at the back door. ☐

3 The wolf knocked at a side door. ☐

4 The wolf pretended to be a baby goat come to play. ☐

5 The kid could see the wolf through the keyhole. ☐

6 The kid was not fooled at all. ☐

One word is not needed 2

Read each sentence. One word need not be in it for the meaning to remain the same. Write the word in the space.

1 A fox chased after the rabbit. ________________

2 The class sat in a round circle. ________________

3 Dad collects old vintage cycles. ________________

4 Never talk to unknown strangers. ____________

5 The two cars collided together. ____________

6 Where was she going to when you met? _____________

7 The two twins wear the same clothes. ________________

8 The sun it shone brightly all day long. _______________

9 At home I have got two pet birds. ________________

10 The wheels of the car sank down in the mud. _____________

11 Do not repeat my secret again to anyone. ________________

12 I hope to stay with my uncle up until Sunday. _____________